CHUCK SMITH

THE MAN GOD USES

14

Characteristics

of a Godly Man

THE WORD
FOR TODAY

P.O. Box 8000 • Costa Mesa, CA 92628 • Web: www.twft.com • E-mail: info@twft.com

THE MAN GOD USES
by Chuck Smith

Published by The Word For Today
P.O. Box 8000, Costa Mesa, CA 92628
(800) 272-WORD (9673)

Web Site: www.twft.com
E-Mail: info@twft.com

© 2003 The Word For Today

ISBN 1-931713-48-0

Printed in the United States of America

The Man God Uses

CHAPTER

1

Let my prayer be set before You as incense,
the lifting up of my hands as the evening sacrifice.

Psalm 141:2

PRAYER

Do you want to be used by God? Do you want your life to count for eternity? Jesus taught us to pray, "Thy will be done on earth as it is in heaven." Are you willing to become an instrument that God can use to accomplish His will here on earth? If so, then it is essential to discover the personal characteristics of the people God used throughout the Scriptures. What made these people so special that God chose to use them?

Just as there are certain characteristics necessary for you to be used by God, there are also opposing characteristics that can disqualify you.

Our lives involve a constant battle between two forces; the Spirit and the flesh. The Apostle Paul vividly describes them in Galatians 5:19-23:

> "Now the works of the flesh are evident, which are: adultery, fornication, uncleanness, licentiousness, idolatry, sorcery, hatred, contentions, jealousies, outbursts of wrath, selfish ambitions, dissensions, heresies, envy, murders, drunkenness, revelries, and the like; of which I tell you beforehand, just as I also told you in time past, that those who practice such things will not inherit the kingdom of God. But the fruit of the Spirit is love, joy, peace, longsuffering, kindness, goodness, faithfulness, gentleness, self-control. Against such there is no law."

When we give in to the enticement of the flesh, we can disqualify ourselves from God's service. Paul warns us in 1 Corinthians 9:27:

> "But I discipline my body and bring it into subjection, lest, when I have preached to others, I myself should become disqualified."

Sadly, many people have disqualified themselves from God's service because they were unable to get their fleshly desires into subjection. Even pastors who have been successfully engaged in ministry for many years have fallen prey to the lusts of the flesh, and they became disqualified for the ministry.

God Uses a Man of Prayer

Now if there are things that can disqualify us from God's service, then logically there are things that are necessary in order for me to be used by God. Notice in Acts 3:1; what were Peter and John doing when they encountered the lame man?

Now Peter and John went up together to the temple at the hour of prayer, the ninth hour (Acts 3:1). They were going to the temple at the hour of prayer. Prayer is the key here. God uses men who maintain regular communion with Him; men who are constantly speaking to, and hearing from God.

Prayer was obviously essential in the life and ministry of the Apostle Paul. In his letter to the church at Thessalonica, he exhorted them to pray without ceasing. Paul often declared that he prayed for the people day and night.

He wrote in Romans 1:9:

> "For God is my witness, whom I serve
> with my spirit in the gospel of His Son,
> that without ceasing I make mention of
> you always in my prayers."

What are the essential components of prayer? How does God's Word teach us that we should pray? Prayer assumes five basic elements: Relationship, worship, confession, petition, and intercession. As we analyze prayers throughout the Scriptures, we see each of these elements regularly demonstrated in the lives of those who pray.

Relationship

The most important aspect of prayer is relationship. "Our Father which art in heaven." Prayer is the privilege of God's children. When God is your Father, you have a right to ask.

Worship

Another important aspect of prayer is worship. Jesus taught us to begin our prayers with worship: "Hallowed be thy name." Peter and John began their prayer in Acts 4:24:

"Lord, You are God, who made heaven
and earth and the sea, and all that is in
them."

They focused on the character of God;
worshiping God for the mighty works He has
done, and standing in awe of their heavenly
Father.

Adoration is an important component of
prayer, because when we realize that we are
speaking with the Living God, the Creator of all
things, our problems are reduced to their proper
perspective. Next to the glorious splendor of the
Almighty God, our problems simply vanish into
insignificance.

We often transfer our human limitations onto
God. What seems easy for me to solve must be easy
for God; what seems difficult or impossible for me
must likewise be difficult or impossible for God.
But when we worship the Lord, we discover that
He is so much greater than our problems.

When my mother was in her final days
suffering from cancer, I went through a wide range
of emotions. The x-rays revealed a growth the size
of a grapefruit blocking her kidneys, which caused
constant excruciating pain. She had an intense

love for the Lord, which made it hard to understand why God would allow her to suffer so much. It was extremely difficult for me to see her in that condition.

One morning, in a moment of emotional anguish, I prayed that God would relieve her from the pain. I asked Him to give me her pain for a single day. The Lord gently reminded me that He had already borne all of her pain.

At that moment, God revealed to me that He is infinitely greater than cancer. I was no longer focusing on a disease that could reduce a perfectly healthy body to a sickly mass of skin and bone. I was standing before the throne of the Almighty God. A few mismanaged cells are nothing compared to the One Who created the entire universe.

At the same moment my mother breathed a sigh of relief and exclaimed, "The pain is gone." Over the next two days, my mother excreted thirty-seven pounds of liquid from her system, as her unblocked kidneys began to function again. Within a week or so, the x-rays showed that the grapefruit-sized growth which had caused her intense pain was completely gone.

She began to sleep almost around the clock, waking up only long enough to say, "Oh, it's so wonderful to not feel pain anymore." As ministers would come over to visit her, they would pray for God to heal her. Then after they would leave, my mother would smile and say to me, "I wasn't agreeing with their prayers. I want to go home to be with the Lord."

So I began to pray for God's will to be done in her life. If God wanted to take her home, I didn't want to prolong her life. Soon afterward, she lapsed into a coma, and the Lord took her home. Sitting at the foot of her bed, I experienced the presence of the Lord in a greater way than I ever had before or since. I felt so near to Him; His voice was so distinct in my heart. Prayer was the natural outgrowth of my relationship with the Lord. As I realized the magnificence of God, I worshiped Him; and as I worshiped Him, I was drawn into His presence. I felt His love and power flowing through me in a new and fresh manner.

Jesus told us in John 4:23:

> "But the hour is coming, and now is, when the true worshipers will worship the Father in spirit and truth; for the Father is seeking such to worship Him."

Worship is the beginning of effective communication with God.

Confession

"Forgive us our debts, as we forgive our debtors" (Matthew 6:12). Although Jesus has already died for every sin we will ever commit – past, present, and future, God still wants us to come to Him when we realize we have sin in our lives. First John 1:9 tells us:

> "If we confess our sins, He is faithful and
> just to forgive us our sins and to cleanse
> us from all unrighteousness."

God already knows every sinful thought, word, and deed we commit, but our confession to Him opens our understanding to the damage that sin brings. David prayed in Psalm 139:23-24:

> "Search me, O God, and know my heart;
> Try me, and know my thoughts; And see
> if there is any wicked way in me, And
> lead me in the way everlasting."

Just as sin grieves the Holy Spirit and hinders our prayer life, confession of sin restores our relationship with the Father, and revitalizes our communication with Him.

Petition

Petition is where we bring our own needs to the Lord. "Give us this day, our daily bread" (Matthew 6:11). People who lack a personal relationship with the Lord often believe that God is too big and too busy to be bothered with their individual needs. This is just thinly-veiled, false humility. God wants us to come to Him with our needs and desires. As the Lord demonstrates His love for us by His bountiful provision in our lives, our relationship with Him matures.

Intercession

"Thy kingdom come, thy will be done in earth as it is in heaven." Finally, our prayers must ultimately move into intercession. We have gone beyond worship, beyond confession, beyond focusing on our own needs, and now we are bringing the needs of others to the Lord's attention. Prayer should always extend beyond myself. If I only pray for my own personal needs, then there is something wrong in my heart.

The life of the Apostle Paul was a model of intercessory prayer. He prayed for everyone with whom the Lord gave him the opportunity to minister, and he even encouraged others to pray for him. Throughout the Bible, God has used men who have relied upon Him with a regular, fervent prayer life.

CHAPTER

2

Then Peter said,
"Silver and gold I do not have,
but what I do have I give you:
In the name of Jesus Christ of Nazareth,
rise up and walk."

Acts 3:6

FAITH

THE KEY TO AN EFFECTIVE PRAYER LIFE is faith in God, who is the Giver of all things. Notice that when Peter approached the lame man, he took him by the right hand and lifted him up, and immediately the man's feet and ankle bones received strength. Put yourself in Peter's position. This man had been lame from birth, and because he sat at the gate of the temple begging for alms every day, he was undoubtedly well known to everyone in the city. Imagine the public scorn Peter would have incurred if he had lifted the man to his feet, only to have the man slump back down onto the ground. Peter would have been a laughing stock all over the city! To obey God in that situation, and to lift the man to his feet must have required an immense amount of faith.

What did Peter say to the man? "In the name of Jesus Christ of Nazareth, rise up and walk" (Acts 3:6). Later, as Peter was explaining the miracle to the astonished crowd at the temple, he said in Acts 3:16, "And His name, through faith in His name, has made this man strong, whom you see and know."

Jesus told us directly in John 14:13:

> "And whatever you ask in My name, that
> I will do, that the Father may be glorified
> in the Son."

Keys To Faith

There is amazing power through faith in the name of Jesus Christ! Where did Peter get the faith to heal the lame man? Notice what Peter said in Acts 3:16b:

> "Yes, the faith which comes through
> Him has given him this perfect
> soundness in the presence of you all."

In other words, Peter is declaring that the Lord not only healed the lame man, but He also gave

Peter the faith to believe that He would do it.

Peter did not claim to have developed the faith through his own spiritual development, or from anything he had done to deserve it; Peter simply told the people that the faith required to do God's work came from God. The Lord just suddenly gave Peter the faith to believe that this lame man could be healed.

As the Apostle Paul is discussing spiritual gifts in 1 Corinthians 12, he specifically mentions the gift of faith. The Bible shows us that in certain instances, God gives people the faith to believe that He is about to do something special in their lives. So, many people attempt to work up their faith for a certain occasion. I believe that this is an exercise in futility.

The key here is that in order to have the faith that assures us God is going to perform a miracle, we must be living in God's will. Notice that Paul tells us in 1 Corinthians 12:11:

> "But one and the same Spirit works all these things, distributing to each one individually as He wills."

The work of the Spirit is done, not according to my will, but according to His will. So the man that

God uses is a man of prayer; a man who walks according to God's will; and a man who has the faith of God to do the work of God.

3

Let your light so shine before men,
that they may see your good works
and glorify your Father in heaven.

Matthew 5:16

GIVE GOD THE GLORY

IT MUST HAVE BEEN A SIGHT TO SEE! The lame man who had been sitting at the gate of the temple begging for alms day after day, literally for decades, was now walking around, leaping into the air, and praising God (Acts 3:8)! Every person in the city had walked by this man over and over again throughout the years, maybe occasionally dropping a coin or two into his hand. His frail frame was undoubtedly a familiar sight, linked with the whole experience of going into the temple in Jerusalem.

All of a sudden one day, this man is dancing around, yelling at the top of his lungs, hugging Peter and John, and generally creating a major disturbance in the daily routine of the temple. The news must have spread like wildfire throughout the crowd! Luke factually states in Acts 3:10, "...they were filled with wonder and amazement at what had happened to him."

The story continues in Acts 3:12:

> "So when Peter saw it, he responded to the people: 'Men of Israel, why do you marvel at this? Or why look so intently at us, as though by our own power or godliness we had made this man walk?'"

In other words, Peter was saying to them, "You men are Israelites! Don't you know the power of your own God? People from foreign countries who aren't acquainted with the God of Abraham, Isaac, and Jacob could conceivably be amazed by this event, but why should you be surprised?"

This is exactly the way we so often behave in the face of miracles, even today. By our own confession, we believe that God created the heavens and the earth and every living creature in them, but when we hear of a quadriplegic walking out of a hospital, it challenges our credulity. Is it any more difficult for God to heal a cripple than it was for Him to create Adam out of the dust of the earth? Do we really believe what we claim to believe?

Dangerous Territory

Although being used as an instrument of God is always a thrilling experience, it is also a potentially dangerous one, since people often tend to exalt the person through whom God works, rather than God Himself. Jesus cautioned us in Matthew 5:16:

> "Let your light so shine before men, that
> they may see your good works and
> glorify your Father in heaven."

Notice, the glory must go to God alone; not to any of us.

The glory of man is such a powerful motivator. Many football players willingly allow their bodies to be maimed for the rest of their lives, just to hear the cheers of the crowd in an instant of time. Just as Satan rebelled against God because of his desire for personal recognition, our own sinful nature craves recognition and glory.

When God answers a man's prayer, people often seek to elevate that man who prayed, as if he had anything at all to do with the results of the prayer. Countless healing ministries all over the United States have turned into big businesses as a result of the response of the masses. Many so-called healers are nothing more than frauds looking to become wealthy off the gullibility of naive people.

The   Instrument   of   God

Several years ago, I met a Christian woman whose husband had resisted coming to the Lord. This man was a prominent psychiatrist and neurosurgeon in the area, and his wife confided in me that while her husband's practice was quite successful, he took his patients' issues so much to heart, that he routinely lost sleep at night. His profound concern for the welfare of his patients was literally destroying his health. Although his careful analysis would reveal to him the precise problem of a given patient, he was tormented by the fact that he was often powerless to actually affect a cure.

This man's wife approached me one day, and asked if my wife, Kay, and I would come over for dinner. The plan was that after dinner, she and Kay would disappear into the kitchen, thus leaving the two of us men to talk alone. After talking with him for several hours over a couple of occasions, I finally confronted him.

"You and I have been sitting here sharing ideas with each other for quite awhile," I said. "I would like your professional analysis of me. I have tried to be as open as possible, and you know that I have a strong faith in Jesus Christ. I believe that the Bible is completely inspired by God, and that every word of it is true. Now, what do you believe I have lost because of my faith in Christ?"

He looked at me and said, "Not a thing. I wish I was as happy as you are. I would love to have the peace and confidence that you have."

Then I added, "What if there really was no God after all, and the Bible was completely false? What have I lost then?"

The answer came back once again, "Nothing. You are about as well-adjusted as anyone I have ever met."

So my next question was this: "Okay, then what if the Bible is true? What have you lost by not believing in Christ as your personal Lord and

Savior?" With that, he surrendered, and we knelt together as he invited Jesus into his heart.

Bright and early the next morning, his wife appeared in my office with a gift for me. She gushed, "Oh Chuck, oh Chuck! I knew you could do it! You are so wonderful!"

I quickly stopped her. "Wait a minute!" I said. "Your husband is one of the top neurosurgeons in the area. Imagine if he had performed an operation where he successfully clipped an aneurysm and saved a man's life. How would he feel if the patient later returned to the hospital, picked up the scalpel used in his operation, and exclaimed, 'Oh what a wonderful scalpel you are! You have the sharpest blade I've ever seen! You are the most glorious piece of steel in the entire world!'?"

We are not supposed to praise the instrument, but rather the One who skillfully uses it to accomplish His purposes. When God uses you, and someone wants to give you the glory, the best thing to do is point them to the One who did the job.

As Peter continued to say in Acts 3:12:

> "...why look so intently at us, as though
> by our own power or godliness we had
> made this man walk?"

Peter was not about to take any credit for what God had done that day. Likewise, the man God uses is a man who is not seeking glory for himself, but seeking only to bring God glory.

4

Who has established all the ends of the earth?
What is His name, and what is His Son's name,
if you know? Every word of God is pure;
He is a shield to those who put their trust in Him.

Proverbs 30:4b-5

GOD'S WORD

IN ACTS CHAPTER THREE, Peter and John were instruments through which God worked a miracle, and all of the people were greatly amazed. They wanted to know what had taken place. Notice that Peter's explanation of Jesus Christ came directly from God's Word.

Peter declared in Acts 3:18,

> "But those things which God foretold by the mouth of all His prophets, that the Christ would suffer, He has thus fulfilled."

Then in Acts 3:21:

> "Whom heaven must receive until the
> times of restoration of all things, which
> God has spoken by the mouth of all His
> holy prophets since the world began."

Peter continued in verse 22, quoting Moses, and then went on to cite the prophetic Scriptures from Samuel to Malachi.

The underlying principle of Peter's declaration here is the recognition that God is the author of the Scriptures. Since God cannot lie, we know that God's Word must be true. Therefore, the ultimate authority we have to explain anything is God's Word.

Notice Peter's statement in Acts 1:16:

> "Men and brethren, this Scripture had to
> be fulfilled, which the Holy Spirit spoke
> before by the mouth of David..."

Since the Holy Spirit spoke through David, then the words of David are the words of God. God's word is inerrant; it simply has to be fulfilled. God help us to become people like Peter who trust in God's Word!

Has God Said?

There is a common tendency today, especially among the intellectually elite, to challenge the Word of God, rather than believe it. Unfortunately, seminaries are constantly disputing the inerrancy of God's Word, instead of discovering what God has communicated to them through His Word. The result of this is the growth of liberalism among the pulpits across the United States. God's Word has been replaced by a lukewarm social gospel. If I did not believe the Bible was God's Word, inspired and inerrant, I would leave the ministry.

The result of this social gospel has been a rapid decline in church membership throughout all of the major denominations. As the older members in the congregation die, church attendance dwindles. Meanwhile, the church continues to drift further away from the radical life-changing truth of God's Word and they have less to offer. Consequently, today's young people avoid going to church, because most denominational churches have become irrelevant to our changing world, while trying to become more relevant by denying God's Word.

On the other hand, churches in which the Bible is believed, taught, and practiced are flourishing.

One element that separates Calvary Chapel from mainstream denominational churches is the emphasis on the verse-by-verse teaching of God's Word; from Genesis through Revelation, and then back to Genesis again.

Renowned for his teaching of God's Word, G. Campbell Morgan was a distinguished Bible expositor and the senior pastor of Westminster Chapel in London during the early part of the twentieth century. From his biography, entitled *The Ministry of the Word,* [1] we find that Morgan's sole reliance upon the pure teaching of the Bible caused thousands of people to flock to his church each week.

Tragically, although Westminster Chapel still exists today, they no longer put an emphasis on teaching God's Word as they did a century ago. When I visited this church one Sunday evening, I counted fewer than thirty people scattered throughout a huge sanctuary—a sanctuary that once overflowed with people standing in the aisles.

---

1. *The Ministry of the Word* by G. Campbell Morgan; 252 pages; Fleming Revel Publishing; published in 1919.

Above His Name

In the ancient Hebrew culture, a man's name was linked to his identity, so the process of naming a child was given essential significance. Throughout the Bible, we see that the name of God is hallowed. As a matter of fact, when Hebrew scribes copied the Scriptures, and they came to the name of God, they were required to set down their pen, take a bath, put on a clean set of clothes, and then get a new pen before they could continue to write.

God's name was considered to be so holy, that they were not even permitted to speak it. With this in mind, notice in the following scripture that God honors His Word even above His name.

> I will worship toward your holy temple, and praise your name for your loving-kindness and your truth; for you have magnified your word above all your name (Psalm 138:2).

Many churches have abandoned the teaching of God's Word in order to emphasize dramatic spiritual experiences in their services. We have seen this precipitated in the "Holy Laughter Movement," beginning with "the Toronto

Blessing," "the Pensacola Blessing," and a myriad of other churches searching for a spectacular phenomenon to lure people into their pews. When a church comes up with a fantastic new sensation, it begins to draw people away from other churches; so the other churches then feel compelled to create something even more exciting to draw the crowds back again.

This type of situation is not new in the church. Notice the Apostle Paul's exhortation in 2 Timothy 4:2-4:

> "Preach the word! Be ready in season and out of season. Convince, rebuke, exhort, with all longsuffering and teaching. For the time will come when they will not endure sound doctrine, but according to their own desires, because they have itching ears, they will heap up for themselves teachers; and they will turn their ears away from the truth, and be turned aside to fables."

If you want to be used by God, then you must be a man who trusts God's Word. The man God uses is a man of the Word.

*So they departed from
the presence of the council,
rejoicing that they were
counted worthy to suffer
shame for His name.*

Acts 5:41

PERSECUTION

T HE FOURTH CHAPTER OF THE BOOK OF ACTS marks the beginning of the persecution against the Church. The Jewish religious leaders had just gotten rid of Jesus; or so they thought! Who were these established religious leaders that came against the early Christians, and what were they trying to accomplish?

Called the Sanhedrin, the governing body of the Jewish religion was made up of two rival sects; the Sadducees and the Pharisees. The Sadducees were pure materialists. They only believed in things that they could experience with their physical senses—and these things did not include angels, spirits, or life after death.

They most certainly did not believe that Jesus rose from the dead. In essence, they were the humanists of their day.

The Pharisees, on the other hand, did believe in life after death. They were more zealous over the law than the Sadducees, and as a result, these two groups were sharply divided on practically every issue.

The Pharisees and the Sadducees had completely different problems with Jesus. Obviously the root of their problems was the fact that Jesus threatened their positions as religious authorities.

The Pharisees

The Pharisees persecuted Jesus because they believed that He broke the Mosaic law. Jesus refused to acknowledge any validity in their man-made traditions. He healed people on the Sabbath, He did not quote the rabbis when He taught, He associated with sinners, and He drew huge crowds everywhere He went.

Worst of all, in their minds, Jesus revealed that He was God.

The Sadducees

The Sadducees' basic problem stemmed from Jesus' teaching on the resurrection of the dead. There is nothing more disturbing to a materialist than being told that when he dies he will go to a place where he cannot take his money. Imagine their dismay when Jesus raised Lazarus from the dead!

The Resurrection

The Sadducees thought that the crucifixion had finally gotten rid of Jesus, but now Peter and John were claiming that Jesus had risen from the dead. On top of that, they were giving Jesus credit for healing the lame man in the temple. As much as they wanted to, the Sadducees couldn't deny this fact, because the proof—the lame man—was walking, talking and praising God in their midst.

The heart of the Gospel, that Jesus has risen from the dead and that He empowers His believers to do the works He did, was staring them in the face.

The teachings of Jesus robbed the Sadducees of their livelihood, something they had achieved by charging people to follow a fabricated religion. If the people believed the message of the Apostles, then the Sadducees' whole industry would come crumbling down. Being materialists, this was intolerable. They were not seeking the truth, they simply wanted to continue with business as usual; in which case, they had to stamp out this teaching of a resurrection.

So, they arrested Peter and John and put them in prison. Luke tells us in Acts 3:1 that it had been about 3:00 in the afternoon when Peter and John went up to the temple, so it was probably about 5:00 p.m. by the time they were thrown into prison. Notice, that in two hours, about five thousand men came to a saving faith in Jesus Christ as a result of the healing of this lame man and Peter's subsequent preaching.

The next day, the Sadducees convened to determine what they could do about this situation. They set Peter and John in front of them, and they asked in Acts 4:7, "By what power or by what name have you done this?"

This was an ingenious leading question designed to trap Peter and John with an Old Testament law from Deuteronomy 13:1-5:

> "If there arises among you a prophet or a
> dreamer of dreams, and he gives you a

sign or a wonder, and the sign or the wonder of which he spoke to you comes to pass, saying, 'Let us go after other gods–which you have not known–and let us serve them,' you shall not listen to the words of that prophet or that dreamer of dreams, for the LORD your God is testing you to know whether you love the LORD your God with all your heart and with all your soul...But that prophet or that dreamer of dreams shall be put to death, because he has spoken in order to turn you away from the LORD your God..."

The healing of the lame man was quite clearly a sign, and everyone in the city was in wonder over it. If Peter and John stuck to their claim that this miracle was performed by Jesus, the Sadducees, interpreting Jesus to be some other god, would then be empowered by God's law to put them to death.

The man God uses must be willing to suffer persecution, even death, for his faith in Jesus Christ.

CHAPTER

6

And when they had prayed,
the place where they were assembled together was shaken;
and they were all filled with the Holy Spirit,
and they spoke the word of God with boldness.

Acts 4:31

SPIRIT-FILLED

IF YOU WANT GOD TO USE YOUR LIFE, you must be filled with the Holy Spirit. Seek the Spirit, walk in the Spirit, be led by the Spirit. These are essential characteristics of people whom God uses.

Peter's answer to the Sadducees put the incident with the lame man into perspective. "We've been arrested, and we are on trial. What are we being examined for? Because a lame man is walking. A good deed has been done." His opening statements reveal the insanity of the whole proceeding. Trials are to determine guilt for an evil deed, not to punish someone for performing an act of kindness.

Then notice how Peter dealt with the Sadducees' trap. He proclaimed in Acts 4:10:

> "Let it be known to you all, and to all the people of Israel, that by the name of Jesus Christ of Nazareth, whom you crucified, whom God raised from the dead, by Him this man stands here before you whole."

Jesus is His name in the Greek language, but in the Hebrew, it is Jehoshua, which means "Jehovah is Salvation." In other words, Peter was declaring, "This miracle was not done by some other god; it was done by Jehovah in the flesh. The same power which raised Jesus, the Messiah of Israel, from the dead, raised this lame man."

Then Peter went on to indict the Sadducees when he quoted Psalm 118:22:

> "This is the 'stone which was rejected by you builders, which has become the chief cornerstone.'"

What Made The Difference?

Not only did Peter avoid their crafty snare, but he turned the tables back on them. Does this sound like the same Peter who was always putting his foot in his mouth when he walked through the Galilean countryside with Jesus? Of course not. Read again Acts 4:8, "Then Peter filled with the Holy Spirit..." Those words 'filled with the Holy Spirit' tell us the difference.

Peter had been transformed by the power of the Holy Spirit. He was literally a different person.

When the Pharisees and the Sadducees constantly attempted to trap Jesus, He always exposed their foolish hearts, and sent them back to their lair, cowering. Peter and John, walking in the power of the Holy Spirit, had that same authority.

The Sadducees knew that they were out-matched. All they could do was offer idle threats, and release Peter and John (Acts 4:13).

God is looking for a man filled with the Holy Spirit, a man whose life has been transformed as he allows the Lord to mold him into the image of Christ.

CHAPTER

7

Nor is there salvation in any other,
for there is no other name under heaven
given among men by which we must be saved.

Acts 4:12

BORN AGAIN

NOTICE PETER'S KNOCK-OUT PUNCH in Acts 4:12. His boldness, coupled with the power of his testimony, was unstoppable. God can use people like that in every walk of life. God is looking for people, especially today, who are willing to boldly proclaim His testimony. There is no other name than Jesus Christ by which we can be saved.

In Matthew 26:36-46, Jesus prayed the same thing three times in the Garden of Gethsemane:

> "O my Father, if it is possible, let this cup pass from Me; nevertheless, not as I will, but as You will."

In other words, Jesus was requesting of the Father, "If there is any way for mankind to be saved from their sins other than by My death on the cross, let it be." The fact that Jesus died on the cross substantiates the fact that there was no other way.

The Only Way

If we could be saved by living a good life, by keeping God's law, or by any other means, then God allowed His only Son to die an excruciatingly painful and humiliating death in vain. The shed blood of Jesus Christ is indeed our only means of salvation. The exclusive nature of the Christian claim is offensive to people, even to the present day.

First of all, it says that we are not acceptable to God as we are. God wants us to come to Him as we are, but we must be willing for Him to transform us into Christ's image. Secondly, there is only one God, and only one mediator between God and man; the man Christ Jesus. This seems to the unregenerate mind to be narrow-minded and intolerant.

In a culture where tolerance is valued above all else, Christianity is falling into disfavor with the intellectual and social elite of the world. The Church is being blamed for obstructing world unity. As the Pope and other religious leaders are working together to form a peaceful world religion, true Christians are standing in the way. In order for them to accomplish their goals, the exclusive claim of Christianity will have to be silenced.

In John 3:3 Jesus said, "Unless one is born again he cannot see the kingdom of God." And then later in John 14:6, He said, "I am the way, the truth, and the life. No one comes to the Father except through Me."

Paul wrote there is one God and one mediator between God and men, the Man Jesus Christ.

Peter responded,

> "Nor is there salvation in any other, for there is no other name under heaven given among men by which we must be saved."

The man God uses is a man who is convinced that salvation and eternal life can only come by being born again through believing in Jesus Christ.

8

*Now when they saw the boldness of Peter and John,
and perceived that they were uneducated
and untrained men, they marveled. And they realized
that they had been with Jesus.*

Acts 4:13

BOLDNESS

PETER'S RESPONSE to the accusatory question of the Sadducees communicated the power of the Holy Spirit. We see in Acts 4:7, that Peter completely turned the tables on them, and laid the guilt squarely upon their shoulders.

In Acts 4:10-12, Peter declares:

> "Let it be known to you all, and to all the people of Israel, that by the name of Jesus Christ of Nazareth, whom you crucified, whom God raised from the dead, by Him this man stands here before you whole. This is the 'stone

which was rejected by you builders, which has become the chief cornerstone.' Nor is there salvation in any other, for there is no other name under heaven given among men by which we must be saved."

The Best Education

The council thought they were talking to uneducated, ignorant fishermen, but in three brief sentences, Peter demonstrated his superior credentials. Peter and John had just graduated from three years of personal tutoring with the greatest Teacher in history. Moreover, the misconception these Sadducees bore is typical of many seminarians today. The question is asked in the Book of Job. "Who by searching can find out God completely?" The truth is that God is not known as the result of an intellectual quest, but by revelation.

Jesus said,

"Nor does anyone know the Father, except the Son, and the one to whom the Son wills to reveal Him" (Matthew 11:27).

Paul wrote:

> "But the natural man does not receive the things of the Spirit of God, for they are foolishness to him; nor can he know them, because they are spiritually discerned" (1 Corinthians 2:14).

People who feed upon God's Word, who have been conformed into the image of Christ, and who are filled with the power of the Holy Spirit are the best guides for the spiritual truth.

There is no better way to learn about God than to walk with Him personally. All the books in the world cannot compare with personal experience.

The response of the Sadducees was priceless.

> Now when they saw the boldness of Peter and John, and perceived that they were uneducated and untrained men, they marveled. And they realized that they had been with Jesus. And seeing the man who had been healed standing with them, they could say nothing against it (Acts 4:13-14).

That was their secret—they had been with Jesus. Nothing can take the place of being with Jesus.

Silencing The Critics

The evidence of Peter and John's divine power was standing right in front of them. What could they say?

Just as God demonstrated His life-changing power to the people in the first century, He has also given us this same power. We see countless examples of people standing in our midst today whom God has healed, not only of physical infirmities, but of mental, emotional, and spiritual conditions as well. God has literally shut the mouths of the skeptics. If they want to deny His power, they must do so in the face of indisputable evidence.

So we read in Acts 4:15-17 that the Sadducees had to huddle together and try to regroup:

> "But when they had commanded them to go aside out of the council, they conferred among themselves, saying, 'What shall we do to these men? For, indeed, that a notable miracle has been done through them is evident to all who dwell in Jerusalem, and we cannot deny it. But so that it spreads no further among the people, let us severely

> threaten them, that from now on they
> speak to no man in this name.'"

Notice the lunacy here. The evidence of God's power was standing right in front of them, but rather than allowing themselves to surrender to the only possible rational conclusion, that Jesus Christ is indeed their Messiah, they willfully chose to suppress the news which was already spreading like wildfire.

The Sanhedrin made three errors in their evaluation of Peter and John. First, their perception that Peter and John were ignorant and unlearned, but in fact they had the wisdom of the Holy Spirit. Second, that they had been with Jesus in the past tense. Jesus was standing with them, but unseen. Their third mistake was thinking that they could quiet these men with mere threats. Peter and John had just recently walked and talked with the resurrected Christ. Jesus had personally commissioned them to preach the Gospel throughout the entire world. There was no question in their minds as to what they should do. They responded in Acts 4:19-20:

> "Whether it is right in the sight of God
> to listen to you more than to God, you

judge. For we cannot but speak the
things which we have seen and heard."

Again, failing to recognize that they were
literally fighting against God Himself, the
Sadducees still refused to surrender. The case was
finally thrown out of court in Acts 4:21:

"So when they had further threatened
them, they let them go, finding no way of
punishing them, because of the people,
since they all glorified God for what had
been done."

Peter and John had just witnessed the results of
Jesus' exhortation from the Sermon on the Mount,
"Let your light so shine before men, that they may
see your good works and glorify your Father in
heaven" (Matt. 5:16). The people were glorifying
God. What a great testimony!

Taking A Stand

American Christians have lived in relative
peace and prosperity for over two hundred years
now, but if the Lord tarries, we will soon find out
what it means to be persecuted for our faith.
Throughout history, the Church has experienced
its greatest growth in the midst of persecution.

Are you willing to stand up for Jesus, even if it means that you and your family will be imprisoned or killed? God is looking for people who will boldly declare His testimony.

When Paul's friends were crying over his decision to go to Jerusalem, although he was warned by the Spirit that bonds and imprisonment awaited him there, he declared, "I am ready, not only to be bound, but to die in Jerusalem for the Lord Jesus."

The man God uses is a man who is bold in his witness for Jesus Christ and will not back down in the face of persecution.

9

Therefore submit to God.

Resist the devil and he will flee from you.

Draw near to God and He will draw near to you.

James 4:7-8a

SUBMITTED TO GOD

WHEN THE COUNCIL finally dismissed Peter and John, they went back to their friends and reported everything that had taken place. The response of the group was a unified prayer of praise to the Lord.

This potent prayer is recorded for us in Acts 4:24-30:

> "Lord, You are God, who made heaven and earth and the sea, and all that is in them, who by the mouth of Your servant David have said: 'Why did the nations rage, and the people plot vain things?

The kings of the earth took their stand,
and the rulers were gathered together
against the Lord and against His Christ.'
For truly against Your holy Servant
Jesus, whom You anointed, both Herod
and Pontius Pilate, with the Gentiles and
the people of Israel, were gathered
together to do whatever Your hand and
Your purpose determined before to be
done. Now, Lord, look on their threats,
and grant to Your servants that with all
boldness they may speak Your word, by
stretching out Your hand to heal, and
that signs and wonders may be done
through the name of Your holy Servant
Jesus."

A Proper Focus

Notice the structure of this prayer. They began
by addressing the Lord, and acknowledging who
He is and what He has done. When you begin a
prayer this way, you put the situation in the
proper perspective. They had just been threatened
by the governing body of the Jewish religion in
Jerusalem, the most powerful men in all of
Judaism at the time. However, in contrast with the

Sovereign Lord of the universe, imposed upon them by this small group disgruntled men meant nothing. As the Aposu. Paul wrote in Ephesians 3:20:

> "[He]...is able to do exceedingly abundantly above all that we ask or think, according to the power that works in us."

Then they quoted from God's Word (Psalm 2). When we focus on the Scriptures as we pray, we are centering our attention on the thoughts of God, rather than on the fears, doubts, and apprehensions which naturally plague our own thinking. As they meditated upon God's Word, they were able to recognize the preeminence of God in the whole situation. God's Word never fails; therefore, as we pray according to His Word, we can be absolutely assured that our prayers are in line with His will, and that we will certainly receive the power we need to accomplish what God has called us to do.

God is in control of every aspect of our life. He knows all about the issues we are facing, and He has known about them since eternity past. There is nothing new to God. He can't be surprised, and we never enter into territory unfamiliar to Him.

Peter and John realized that God knew all about their situation. He had known about it for over a thousand years, so He inspired David to write about it. What David wrote about happened to them on that day.

Likewise, when Jesus commissioned His followers to make disciples of all the nations, He knew exactly what that would entail. He already knew about the threats of the Sanhedrin. As we pray according to God's will, we are submitting to Him and centering our hearts on His power, which enables our faith to be put into action.

Notice that although the petition of their prayer was for boldness and power to speak God's Word, they did not immediately offer their own concerns and requests, but they fixed their hearts on the Person of God. This very relationship gave them the boldness they needed to deal with the threats they had just received from the Sanhedrin.

There is nothing more powerful than prayer which is aligned with God's will.

What would you do if they passed a law prohibiting Christian evangelization in the United States? This may come to pass sooner than you think. Do you have the boldness to obey God rather than man, regardless of the consequences?

A Powerful Answer

Notice the results when the disciples prayed according to God's will. Acts 4:31 tells us:

> "And when they had prayed, the place where they were assembled together was shaken; and they were all filled with the Holy Spirit, and they spoke the word of God with boldness."

Their prayer was answered. Now look at the results. Acts 4:33 reports:

> "And with great power the apostles gave witness to the resurrection of the Lord Jesus. And great grace was upon them all."

God showed His love, grace, and mercy through the miracles that were manifested in His believers; thus proving that Jesus did in fact rise from the dead, and that He has the power to save anyone who would come to Him by faith, both then and now.

The man God uses is a man who is wholly submitted unto the will of God.

For as many as are led by the Spirit of God,

these are the sons of God.

Romans 8:14

SPIRIT-LED

Acts 4:32-37 DESCRIBES the financial arrangement of the early Church in Jerusalem: Everyone shared what they had with the entire group. If someone had a need, it was provided for him from a common fund. Individual property and possessions were voluntarily set aside by each person in the group. Initially, there were no problems with this situation.

Undoubtedly, part of the motivation for this living arrangement was their belief in the imminent return of Christ. "Why should I care about my property here on earth, when I'll be in heaven soon? After all, it's all going to burn anyhow."

Notice, there is nothing in the Scriptures that commanded them to sell their property and give it to the Church. Luke just states that the people sold their property, and brought the proceeds to the apostles, who then distributed to each according to their need. Although this was all done voluntarily, you can see how the people got caught up in the fervor; and soon everyone was involved—even though it may not have been guided by the Holy Spirit. It simply became the thing to do.

The Spirit or the Flesh?

This is a perfect example of how something spiritual can turn into something fleshly in a hurry. As people in the church brought huge sums of money to the apostles, their contributions were noticed by the rest of the church. It became the "spiritual" thing to do.

Soon, people were making contributions just to gain the attention of the group, which became tremendously gratifying to the flesh. We must carefully guard against this type of fleshly gratification in our own lives.

This is one of the problems with many of the so-called revivals in the Church today. Take the "Holy Laughter" movement, for example. When people roll on the floor laughing, they draw attention to themselves, and severely disrupt the service. The attention of the congregation is taken off the teaching of God's Word, and then becomes focused on an individual who is behaving erratically. On the surface, the whole practice can seem deeply spiritual; however, under closer scrutiny, it is actually a means of glorifying the flesh.

I personally believe that when the early believers in Jerusalem put all their possessions into a common fund, they were making a mistake. In the very next chapter of Acts, we see the first problem. Ananias and Sapphira were so anxious to be recognized for their generosity, that they lied to the Holy Spirit and they were then killed by God.

We see further problems, in Acts 6, when a division arose between the Jews and the Hellenists over the distribution of finances to the widows. The ultimate result, of course, was that they eventually went bankrupt, and the Apostle Paul had to take up a collection from the Gentile churches in order to provide for the poor brethren in Jerusalem.

Learning Our Lessons

Unfortunately, other groups throughout Church history have failed to learn the lesson from the first century church, and they have fallen into the same plight. In the 1800's, a group, known as the Millerites, sold their belongings, put on white robes, and gathered together to wait for the Lord's coming. Their leader, Reverend William Miller, felt that God had revealed to him, through a gross misinterpretation of the book of Daniel, that Jesus was coming back on a certain day. Many of these people suffered not only financial disaster, but spiritual disaster as well.

The Jehovah's Witnesses have set all sorts of dates on the coming of the Lord, which turned out to be incorrect, and all those following their advice were hurt by a lack of spiritual discernment. Most recently, there was a sixteen-year-old Korean young man who predicted that Jesus was coming back. He convinced many people in the Korean community to sell everything they owned and then give the money to him. He subsequently ended up in prison for fraud. I would heartily recommend that you make certain of the leading of the Holy Spirit in your life.

The man God uses is a man who is led by the Holy Spirit.

11

So, as much as is in me, I am ready
to preach the gospel to you who are in Rome also.
For I am not ashamed of the gospel of Christ...

Romans 1:15-16a

UNCOMPROMISING

ACTS 5 BEGINS WITH THE ACCOUNT of Ananias and Sapphira. This couple conspired together to sell a plot of land, and then donate only a portion of the proceeds to the church, while claiming that they were giving everything they had. Because of this, God struck them both dead on the spot. Now the important thing for us to consider is this: What was the sin of Ananias and Sapphira?

Notice Peter's statement in Acts 5:3-4:

> "Ananias, why has Satan filled your heart to lie to the Holy Spirit and keep back part of the price of the land for

yourself? While it remained, was it not your own? And after it was sold, was it not in your own control? Why have you conceived this thing in your heart? You have not lied to men but to God."

What Went Wrong?

God did not demand Ananias and Sapphira to give everything they had to the church. Their sin was not that of selfishness or greed; of holding back from the church. In fact, they were not required to give anything at all to the church. Their sin was hypocrisy. They were trying to deceive the congregation into thinking that they were more spiritual than they actually were.

Throughout history, we find that the Holy Spirit functions in an atmosphere of purity. If we want the Holy Spirit to work in our lives, then the first step we must take is repentance for our sins. When we allow the Lord to cleanse us from all unrighteousness, then we open the door for Him to work in our lives, and subsequently, in the life of the Church. However, the moment hypocrisy begins to creep into the Church—caused by man's desire to receive glory—the atmosphere is polluted and the work of God is hindered.

The Separation of Death

Luke's account here in Acts 5 tells us that Ananias and Sapphira fell down and breathed their last; or in King James English, they "gave up the ghost." When a person stops breathing, oxygen is no longer being transported to the brain. If the brain ceases to function, we consider the person to be legally dead. However, a more basic definition of death in the Bible is "separation." Physical death is the separation of a person's consciousness from his body; and spiritual death is the separation of a person's consciousness from God.

If a person is living without the consciousness of God, then—from a spiritual standpoint—that person is dead. The person who is spiritually dead has no communion with God. He has no place in his heart or mind to seek after God, or even to think about God, and Paul tells us in 1 Timothy 5:6 that this person is dead while he still lives. Paul also tells us in Ephesians 2:1 that when we come to Christ by faith, we are made alive. Moreover, Jesus promised in John 11:25-26:

> "I am the resurrection and the life. He
> who believes in Me, though he may die,
> he shall live. And whoever lives and
> believes in Me shall never die."

In other words, whoever believes in Christ will never be consciously separated from God. So a person can be (spiritually) dead while they are (physically) alive, but a person can also be (spiritually) alive after they are (physically) dead.

Jesus taught in John 3 that in order for us to enter into the kingdom of heaven, we must be born again. We obviously must be born physically, but then at some point in our lives, we must also be born spiritually to have eternal life. Due to the original sin of mankind, passed down through the generations from Adam, we are born spiritually dead. In order to gain the relationship with God that Adam threw away, we must undergo a spiritual birth, which is to be "born again." So there are, in essence, two births and two deaths. If you are born twice, you will only die once; but if you are born only once, you will die twice. As the resurrected Christ warned us in Revelation 21:8:

> "But the cowardly, unbelieving, abominable, murderers, sexually immoral, sorcerers, idolaters, and all liars shall have their part in the lake which burns with fire and brimstone, which is the second death."

The Nature of the Spirit

Notice one other component in the account of Ananias and Sapphira. Peter inquired in Acts 5:3-4, "Ananias, why has Satan filled your heart to lie to the Holy Spirit...? You have not lied to men but to God." There are two distinct truths we can observe from this passage. First, the Holy Spirit is God. He is one of the three Persons of the triune Godhead, and this is one of many Scriptures which distinctly states that fact. So if someone tells you that the doctrine of the Trinity is a manmade belief, that it is not found in the Bible, these verses clearly refute such a foolish idea.

The second observation we can make here is the fact that the Holy Spirit is a Person, not an impersonal force, as many people mistakenly teach. Notice that Ananias had lied to the Holy Spirit. It would be silly for me to state that I lied to gravity, or that I lied to electricity, because I cannot lie to an impersonal force. The Holy Spirit is God, and we can have a personal relationship with Him.

A Serious Faith

What were the results of God striking Ananias and Sapphira dead on the spot? Acts 5:11 simply states, "So great fear came upon all the church and upon all who heard these things."

People got serious about their relationship with God, and as a result, the Holy Spirit performed tremendous miracles among them. The news spread and people came to faith in Christ by the thousands. Then, as is typical of non-believers when God begins to move among His people, the Sadducees became nervous. Once again, they hauled the apostles into court for more questions and threats.

We read, beginning in Acts 5:18, that they took all of the apostles and threw them into prison. But at night, an angel opened the prison doors and let them out, commanding them to go into the temple and tell all of the people what had happened. When the high priests summoned the apostles the next morning, the officers came back with the report that even though the prison door was locked, and the guards were all standing outside the cell, the prison was empty.

Luke relates in Acts 5:25:

> "So one came and told them, saying, 'Look, the men whom you put in prison are standing in the temple and teaching the people!'"

Imagine what the high priest was thinking at that point!

Notice the charge laid against the apostles in Acts 5:28:

> "Did we not strictly command you not to teach in this name? And look, you have filled Jerusalem with your doctrine, and intend to bring this Man's blood on us!"

The high priests were concerned, that due to the preaching of the Gospel, the guilt for the blood of Christ would be heaped upon their heads. This was a complete reversal from their earlier statement to Pontius Pilate when they were trying to have Jesus crucified. There they said, "His blood be on us and on our children" (Matthew 27:25).

Once again, the Sadducees charged the apostles to stop preaching the Gospel; and once again, the apostles replied that they had to obey God rather than man. They let the Sadducees know, in no uncertain terms, what their priorities were.

What are your priorities? Are you compelled to obey God rather than man, or do you make compromises according to the dictates of this world? The man God uses is uncompromising.

12

But Peter and the other apostles answered and said:
"We ought to obey God rather than men."

Acts 5:29

OBEDIENT

THE COUNCIL PROBED THE APOSTLES in Acts 5:28, "Did we not strictly command you not to teach in this name?" And Peter responded in Acts 5:29, "We ought to obey God rather than men." The phrase "ought to" used there in the English text is more accurately translated from the Greek language "must." It is a divine imperative. The call of God is far more important than the dictates of willfully unbelieving people.

Jesus Christ has commissioned each and every disciple of His, from the time He ascended until the time He returns, to proclaim the Gospel throughout the world. He even told us that people were not going to receive the message; that we would be persecuted for simply delivering it. Can you declare with Peter, "I must obey God rather than men."? This is indeed a divine imperative.

Peter went on in Acts 5:30-32:

> "The God of our fathers raised up Jesus whom you murdered by hanging on a tree. Him God has exalted to His right hand to be Prince and Savior, to give repentance to Israel and forgiveness of sins. And we are His witnesses to these things, and so also is the Holy Spirit whom God has given to those who obey Him."

Jesus told us in Luke 11:13 that our heavenly Father will give the Holy Spirit to those who ask Him. Now we read here in Acts 5:32 that God gives the Holy Spirit to those who obey Him.

Reaction to the Message

Acts 5:33 reveals the reaction of the high priests to Peter's bold declaration: "When they heard this, they were furious, and plotted to kill them." The conviction of the Holy Spirit will do interesting things to people.

To some, it brings repentance; to others, it brings indignation and rage. The same sun which melts wax, also hardens clay. These men were so furious with the message, that they wanted to kill the messengers.

So they put the apostles outside the courtroom while they discussed among themselves what should be done. A Pharisee by the name of Gamaliel, an expert lawyer who was respected by all, stood up to speak. He could see that the council had ceased to think rationally. They were so riled up, that they literally were ready to tear the apostles to pieces. Although Gamaliel himself was not yet a believer in Christ, his message contained simple, but profound truth.

He began by reminding the men that self-proclaimed messiahs had come and gone throughout the preceding years. He continued in Acts 5:38-39:

> "And now I say to you, keep away from these men and let them alone; for if this plan or this work is of men, it will come to nothing; but if it is of God, you cannot overthrow it–lest you even be found to fight against God."

The Surrender of Saul

Saul of Tarsus, the man who later became the Apostle Paul, was personally tutored by Gamaliel; and since Saul was also a Pharisee, he was most likely in attendance during this occasion. We know Saul's extreme contempt for the Gospel message from Luke's account in Acts 6, when Saul consented with the council which stoned Stephen. Shortly thereafter, Saul traveled to Damascus, where he planned to arrest more followers of Christ. However, on his way, we read in Acts 9, that Jesus appeared to him in a blinding light. As Saul fell to the ground, he heard the voice of Jesus say to him, "Saul, Saul, why are you persecuting Me?" Saul responded with two questions. First, "Who are you, Lord?" and then, upon hearing the answer "Jesus," he asked, "What would you have me to do, Lord?"

At last, Saul understood Gamaliel's statement, "If this is of God, you cannot overthrow it; lest you even be found to fight against God." Fortunately, Saul surrendered his will to Jesus; so that at the end of his life, he could triumphantly proclaim in 2 Timothy 4:7-8:

> "I have fought the good fight, I have finished the race, I have kept the faith.

Finally, there is laid up for me the crown of righteousness, which the Lord, the righteous Judge, will give to me on that Day..."

A Privilege To Suffer

Once again, the council commanded the apostles to stop preaching Christ; they again threatened them, and this time, they beat them. How did the apostles respond to this? They rejoiced that God had counted them worthy to suffer shame for the name of Jesus, and they continued to preach to anyone who would listen. Notice the difference our attitudes can make in various situations. Rather than backing down, the apostles considered the physical pain and public humiliation a blessing. God will mightily use people with this kind of attitude.

The man God uses is obedient to his Lord, Jesus Christ.

13

And the Lord said, "Who then is that faithful
and wise steward, whom his master will make ruler over
his household, to give them their portion
of food in due season?"
Luke 12:42

GOOD
STEWARD

LUKE RECORDS FOR US in Acts 6:1:

> "Now in those days, when the number of
> the disciples was multiplying, there
> arose a murmuring against the Hebrews
> by the Hellenists, because their widows
> were neglected in the daily
> distribution."

Who were the Hebrews and the Hellenists; and
why were they quarreling? The Hellenists were
Jews who followed the Grecian culture. The
Hebrews adhered more strictly to the orthodox
Jewish culture.

There were no major theological differences between these two groups. They just followed different cultures.

The Hellenists complained because they felt that their widows were being neglected. Remember, a major problem the Jerusalem Christians experienced was the administrative burden of distributing common funds to needy individuals in the church; and as time went on, the complexities of this endeavor grew. When the apostles realized that this problem was taking too much of their time, they called a church meeting.

An Age-Old Problem

The apostles were called by God to teach the Word of God, not to referee every little squabble in the church. Something had to be done to allow those called to be pastors, teachers, and evangelists to do their jobs unto the Lord. Their solution was the establishment of the first board of deacons.

This is a problem in the Church today, especially in small churches all over the country. People in these small congregations often expect the pastor to cater to their every need. When I pastored small churches, I was called upon to visit the sick, to counsel those with marital problems, and to serve as a taxi service for widows and shut-ins. While these activities are necessary, they robbed the church of a pastor who was thoroughly prepared to teach the Word of God each week.

Pastors are human beings too, and they have only twenty-four hours in each day. If the senior pastor fills his time with church administration, he won't have time for prayer, study, or sermon preparation.

In addition, much of the time spent in counseling is a result of people who neglect their personal prayer life—these same people generally neglect reading their Bible, fellowshiping with other believers, and paying close attention to the weekly studies from the pulpit.

The Best Counselor

Years ago, one of my assistant pastors created a list of tape numbers that correlated with various issues. Whenever a person finished pouring out their long, sad story, he would just say, "You need tape number 5622. Go over to the bookstore and get it. Next!"

Although on the surface, this type of approach may seem callous or uncaring, the fundamental principle here is the fact that God's Word is our best counselor. The Apostle Paul made the statement to the Ephesian elders in Acts 20:26-27:

> "Therefore I testify to you this day that I
> am innocent of the blood of all men. For
> I have not shunned to declare to you the
> whole counsel of God."

Here at Calvary Chapel, we teach God's word, verse by verse, chapter by chapter, from Genesis to Revelation; the whole counsel of God. Every single issue in life is covered by the Scriptures. If you diligently study the whole Word of God, you will lack nothing.

Keeping Priorities

Through this difficulty in the First Century church, the apostles recognized that the priority of their calling was twofold: Prayer and the ministry of the Word. So they appointed seven men of good reputation, full of the Holy Spirit and wisdom to preside over the administration of the church. The apostles commissioned these first seven deacons by praying and laying hands on them. The laying on of hands for those called to undertake a church ministry is a beautiful custom that we still practice today.

The man God uses is a man who is a good steward over the things that God has entrusted to him.

14

*"Blessed is that servant whom his master
will find so doing when he comes."*

Luke 12:43

FAITHFUL SERVANT

NOTICE WHAT HAPPENED in Acts 6:7: "Then the word of God spread, and the number of the disciples multiplied greatly in Jerusalem..." God has ordained that by feeding on His Word, His flock is strengthened; and then healthy sheep beget healthy sheep. In other words, God increases His flock by multiplication, not just by addition.

Also notice, however, that in this case, before God could multiply, He first had to subtract. It was absolutely necessary for the long-term health of the church that God remove Ananias and Sapphira. Then and only then could He bless the church with multiplication. God is not interested in large numbers; He wants us to be a powerful, dynamic Church, which is focused solely on Him. If there are people in the ministry who are trying to divide the church, God wants to either bring them to repentance or get them out. So do not mourn when God performs a subtraction; just look for God's multiplication in the near future.

Small Things Matter

Seven men were chosen to wait on tables, to distribute the welfare, and just generally to manage all of the minute details in the operation of the church. Our church today needs many people of this capacity; janitors, parking attendants, ushers, secretaries, receptionists, Sunday school teachers, counselors, prayer warriors, and more. While these positions may seem menial to some, they are all absolutely necessary for the smooth functioning of the church.

If God has called you to be a janitor, then follow Paul's exhortation in Colossians 3:17, "Whatever you do in word or deed, do all in the name of the Lord Jesus, giving thanks to God the Father through Him." Cleaning up trash around the church is a ministry to the Lord; and if we do it as such, we are blessed by the Lord the same as someone who preaches the Gospel.

The interesting thing, though, is that when a person works faithfully unto the Lord as a janitor, he rarely remains a janitor. Many men who were once janitors at our church are now the senior pastors of their own churches. If we are faithful to the Lord in small things, then He will raise us up into even greater areas of responsibility.

Later in the book of Acts, we read about two of the seven deacons, Stephen and Philip, whom God raised up to preach His Word. God used Stephen to deliver a message which was so powerful, and so convicting, that his audience stoned him to death before he could even finish his sermon.

God gave Stephen, a former waiter of tables, the distinction of being the first Christian martyr. Likewise, Philip became one of the great first century evangelists. In fact, we read in the eighth chapter of Acts that God called Philip out of a major revival in Samaria to share the Gospel with a eunuch, who happened to be reading the scrolls of Isaiah on his way back to his homeland in Ethiopia. The man came to faith in Christ, got baptized out in the desert, went back home, and shared the Gospel with his fellow countrymen. History tells us that thousands of people all over northern Africa came to the Lord because of this man's testimony.

So God uses people who are willing to serve Him in small things. The man God uses is faithful.

*So they departed from the presence of the council,
rejoicing that they were counted worthy to suffer
shame for His name. And daily in the temple,
and in every house, they did not cease teaching
and preaching Jesus as the Christ.*

Acts 5:41-42

THE MAN GOD USES

WHAT KIND OF MAN DOES GOD USE? God uses the man who comes to the cross daily; who has no ambitions for himself. God uses the man whose life brings honor and glory to Christ. God is looking for the person who refuses to seek after the applause of men; who, like Jesus, is centered on submission to God's will. He is looking for that person who is willing to present his body as a living sacrifice, holy and acceptable to God.

Are You Willing?

We are living in the last days before Jesus

returns for His bride, and I believe that God wants to give this world one final witness of His love, grace, and mercy before His righteous judgment comes. The prophet Joel spoke of the former rain and the latter rain (Joel 2:23); and I am praying that the Lord would pour out His Spirit all over the world, that we would see genuine revival—not in a "circus" atmosphere which brings attention to man—but in a genuine manner that draws people to Jesus Christ.

Since Adam's original sin, God has been looking for a man that He can use to accomplish His purposes. Genesis 5:24 tells us the simple testimony of such a man: "And Enoch walked with God."

When your life here on earth comes to an end, do you want to be known as a person who walked with God? Are you willing to allow the Holy Spirit to take control of your life right now? During the time of Ezekiel, God searched for a man who would stand in the gap between Himself and the sinful nation of Israel.

Will you be that type of man?

We catch a glimpse of God's heavenly glory in Isaiah 6, when Isaiah entered into

God's presence. Isaiah recorded in verse 8:

> "I heard the voice of the Lord, saying:
> 'Whom shall I send, and who will go for
> Us?' Then I said, 'Here am I! Send me.'"

Do you want God to use your life? Are you willing to say with Isaiah, "Here am I, Lord! Send me."? If so, then it's time to strap on your spiritual armor, pick up your sword, and get in the battle.

For the man God uses is willing to be used.

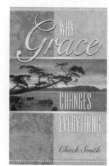

THE FINAL CURTAIN
This recently updated book deals with such subjects as Bible prophecy, the Middle East, Russia, and the role of the Antichrist. Also included is a helpful glossary with terms relating to the Bible and prophecy. 96 pages.

THE GOSPEL
ACCORDING TO GRACE
A clear and enlightening commentary on the Book of Romans. Chuck Smith reviews Paul's epistle, one of the most important books in the Bible, on a verse-by-verse basis. 231 pages.

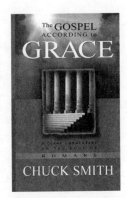

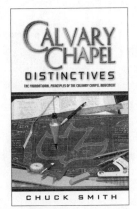

CALVARY CHAPEL
DISTINCTIVES
Calvary Chapel values both the teaching of God's Word, as well as the work of the Holy Spirit. It is this balance that makes Calvary Chapel a distinct and uniquely blessed movement of God. 250 pages.

EFFECTIVE PRAYER LIFE
This practical study in prayer will
equip and help you to have a more
effective and dynamic prayer life. An
excellent resource for personal growth and
group discipleship. 99 pages.

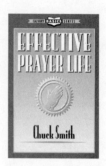

HARVEST
Pastors from ten Calvary Chapels share
how God broke through the barriers of
evil, pride, and anger to carry out His
plan. Many insights into evangelizing
and trusting God's Word make this book
a valuable resource for every believer.
160 pages.

TRIBULATION AND THE CHURCH
Will the church of Christ experience the
Tribulation? This book expounds upon
biblical prophecy and future events while
looking at the role the church will play.
72 pages.

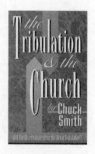

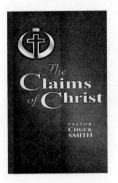

THE CLAIMS OF CHRIST
Chuck Smith gives a straightforward presentation of the claims of Jesus Christ, along with proof of their validity. Readers are challenged to accept or reject the claims of Christ. 16 pages.

WHAT THE WORLD IS COMING TO
This book is a complete commentary on the book of Revelation and the scenario for the last days. Our world is coming to an end fast, but you don't have to go down with it! 215 pages.

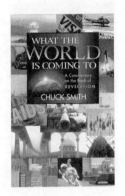

1 JOHN NOTES
Excellent for pastors or students! Taken from Chuck Smith's personal study notes, this can be used as an outline for Bible study groups, Sunday school classes, or individual studies. First John is explored verse-by-verse, with cross-referencing to other books of the Bible. 66 pages.

TO ORDER CALL 1-800-272-WORD (9673)

**COMFORT
FOR THOSE WHO MOURN**
In this pamphlet, Pastor Chuck shares
the glorious hope we have in the
resurrection of Jesus Christ and how
we can find comfort through Him
during a time of loss. 15 pages.

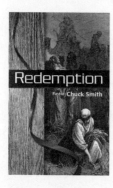

REDEMPTION
In this clear and easy to read commentary,
Pastor Chuck explores and explains the
concept of our redemption in Christ using
as background the story of Ruth and her
"Goel" or savior, Boaz.
16 pages.

**CHRISTIAN FAMILY
RELATIONSHIPS**
Christian Family Relationships reveals
God's basic principles designed to keep
your family's love alive. By knowing and
applying God's principles to your family
life, you can have real peace and joy.
68 pages.

CHARISMA VS. CHARISMANIA
Chuck Smith explores the "charismatic experience," a theological controversy that has existed for years. A wonderful book for those seeking to find a balanced relationship with the Holy Spirit. 146 pages.

THE SEARCH FOR MESSIAH
Written by Dr. Mark Eastman & Chuck Smith, this book is a gateway of discovery for the serious pilgrim in search of the Messiah. The skeptic will be challenged and the Christian deeply enriched. 276 pages.

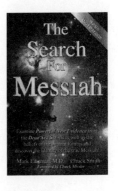

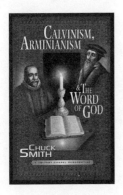

CALVINISM, ARMINIANISM
& THE WORD OF GOD
This pamphlet discusses the facts upon which these two doctrinal stands are based, and compares them to the Word of God. 8 pages.

TO ORDER CALL 1-800-272-WORD (9673)

THE MAN GOD USES
In his warm personal style, Chuck Smith examines the Book of Acts, bringing the Scriptures to life with engaging illustrations and practical wisdom. "The Man God Uses" will lead you into a deeper spiritual walk, while helping you to understand God's purpose and plan for your life. 144 pages.

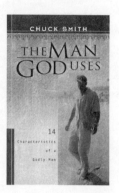

HOW CAN A MAN BE BORN AGAIN?
Pocket-sized and perfect for witnessing, this pamphlet explains what it means to be born again and why it is crucial if you want to see the kingdom of God. Includes a sinner's prayer. 24 pages. Also available in Spanish.

OTHER PRODUCTS BY CHUCK SMITH:

M P 3

PASTOR CHUCK SMITH
THROUGH THE BIBLE
C-2000 SERIES ON MP3
Using an MP3 format, The Word
For Today put Pastor Chuck
Smith's entire C-2000 series on a
set of 8 CD's. You can now fit the
complete audio of Pastor Chuck's
Old and New Testament Bible
studies into your purse or pocket.

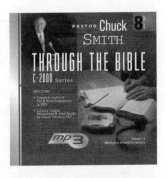

You can play these CD's on your computer or an MP3 player.
Macintosh & Windows compatible.

COMPUTER SYSTEM REQUIREMENTS:
Windows 95, 98, 2000, NT:
- Pentium or higher • 4x CD-ROM drive or faster
- 32 MB of RAM or higher • Sound card
- 25 MB of free hard disk space (if software is to be installed)

Macintosh PowerPC:
- Mac OS 8.1 or later • 32 MB of RAM or higher
- 25 MB of free hard disk space (if software is to be installed)
- 4x CD-ROM drive or faster

SOFTWARE
Windows 95/98/2000/NT
Macintosh PowerPC
- Adobe Acrobat Reader 4.0 • RealPlayer 8

MP3 PLAYER REQUIREMENTS:
- Must be able to play 32KB files

TO ORDER CALL 1-800-272-WORD (9673)

By Chuck Smith:
AUDIO RESOURCES

GOD'S WAKE UP CALL TAPE PACK
Beginning with a heartfelt prayer
delivered by Pastor Chuck on Sept. 11,
2001, this tape pack will help
the listener understand God's
purpose and plan for our nation.
6 messages.

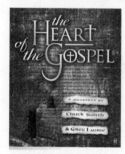

THE HEART OF THE GOSPEL
TAPE OR CD PACK
Have you ever wondered what it
means to be born again or why Jesus'
resurrection is crucial to the Christian
faith? Maybe you wanted to share your
faith with others, but weren't sure how.
By Pastors Chuck Smith & Greg Laurie.
4 messages. Available on cassette or CD.

ISRAEL TAPE
PACK
This tape pack studies the richness
of the Hebrew culture and homeland;
from their feasts to their covenants
with God. Ten biblical studies by
Pastor Chuck Smith, Chuck Missler,
Brian Brodersen, Dave Hunt,
and David Hocking.
10 messages.

TO ORDER CALL 1-800-272-WORD (9673)

SIGNS OF HIS COMING TAPE PACK
This series examines current events as they relate to end times. Drawing from Bible studies in the books of Daniel, Matthew, Revelation and Zechariah, Pastor Chuck explains prophecy in light of today's changing world. 4 messages.

THE BOOK OF REVELATION
TAPE OR CD PACK
These messages will help the listener understand one of the most enigmatic and prophetic books of the Bible. Pastor Chuck explains and dissects Revelation, chapter by chapter - the only book of the Bible that declares a blessing on those who read or hear it. 7 messages. Available on audio cassette or CD.

PROPHECY UPDATE TAPE PACK
What are the implications of the recent events in Israel? Are the pieces of the puzzle finally coming together, leading to a one-world government? Pastor Chuck examines these issues in a timely series. In-depth commentaries on prophetic Scripture passages are also included. 4 messages

TO ORDER CALL 1-800-272-WORD (9673)

MARRIAGE & FAMILY TAPE PACK
Volumes 1 & 2
Discusses the blessing of personal relationships, how to mend bad relationships, the importance of training our children, and scriptural duties of husbands and wives.
Volume 1 has 6 messages.
Volume 2 has 7 messages.

MY REDEEMER LIVES TAPE PACK
This collection of 8 tapes contains 14 Old & New Testament Bible studies. It covers the death and resurrection of Jesus Christ: From the fulfillment of prophetic scriptures to the proof of the resurrection. 14 messages.

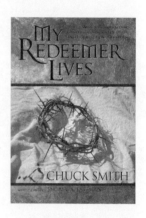

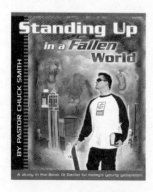

STANDING UP IN A FALLEN WORLD TAPE PACK
Based on the Book of Daniel, these messages were recorded during a youth camp. Each tape contains a powerful message for today's young generation. Suitable for those between the ages of 12 - 20. A study guide is also available.

TO ORDER CALL 1-800-272-WORD (9673)

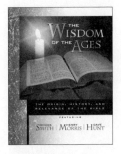

THE WISDOM OF THE AGES
TAPE PACK
Pastor Chuck Smith, Dr. Henry Morris,
and Dave Hunt discuss the most reliable
Bible translations, the basis for our Bible,
as well as the inerrancy, sufficiency, and
authority of the scriptures.
4 messages.

A SERVANT'S HEART TAPE PACK
Whether you teach Sunday school to a
classroom of five-year olds, or lead
worship for a congregation of five
thousand, the Lord has a special plan for
your life. This tape pack focuses on the
nature of a servant, as well as the
requirements necessary to follow the Lord.
7 messages.

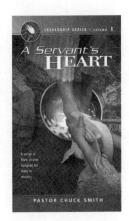

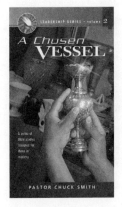

A CHOSEN VESSEL
TAPE PACK
How can we better prepare ourselves
to be used by the Lord? This tape pack
encourages and guides those in ministry,
preparing them for the work set before
them. This collection focuses on the tools
necessary to be a leader.
7 messages.

TO ORDER CALL 1-800-272-WORD (9673)

MOST REQUESTED TAPE PACK
This tape pack contains twelve of the most requested Bible studies by Pastor Chuck. Some messages included are: Faith that prevails; How can a man be born again; Trusting in lies, and How long 'til the end.
12 messages.

2001 CALVARY CHAPEL MEN'S CONFERENCE TAPE PACK
Well-known Calvary Chapel pastors address a wide variety of topics that pertain to "staying on course." Speakers include: Chuck Smith, Jon Courson, Raul Ries, David Rosales, Steve Mays, Brian Brodersen, and Pancho Juarez.
7 messages.

CREATION VS. EVOLUTION TAPE PACK
Pastor Chuck Smith hosts a collection of biblical studies that focus on the validity of Creation and the scientific evidence that backs it up. Joining Pastor Chuck are guest speakers; Chuck Missler, Roger Oakland, Dr. Mark Eastman and Dr. Henry Morris.
10 messages.

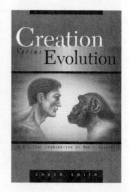

TO ORDER CALL 1-800-272-WORD (9673)

THE PERSON OF THE HOLY SPIRIT TAPE PACK

This set explains who the Holy Spirit is and how He works. 12 messages.

THE GIFTS OF THE HOLY SPIRIT TAPE PACK

This tape pack covers such subjects as miracles, healing, prophecy, faith and speaking in tongues.
19 messages.

THE ARMOR OF GOD

Recorded during the 2002 Calvary Chapel Men's Conference, these messages deal with spiritual warfare. Speakers include: Chuck Smith, David Rosales, Greg Laurie, Jeff Johnson, Raul Ries, Steve Mays, Bob Coy, Don McClure, Pancho Juarez, and Jon Courson. 10 messages. Available on audio tape, CD, or MP3.

FOR MEN ONLY

A series of messages that deal with the issues men struggle with as they seek to live godly lives. Speakers include: Chuck Smith, Jon Courson, Damian Kyle, Bob Coy, Don McClure, Mike MacIntosh, Louis Neely, Gayle Erwin, Sandy Adams, Ricky Ryan, Steve Mays and Joe Sabolick. 12 messages. Available on audio tape, CD, or MP3.

TO ORDER CALL 1-800-272-WORD (9673)

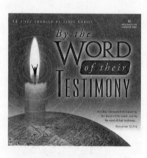

To order any of our products or to
receive a free catalog,
please call us at
1-800-272-WORD

Or write to us at
THE WORD FOR TODAY
P.O. Box 8000
Costa Mesa, CA 92628